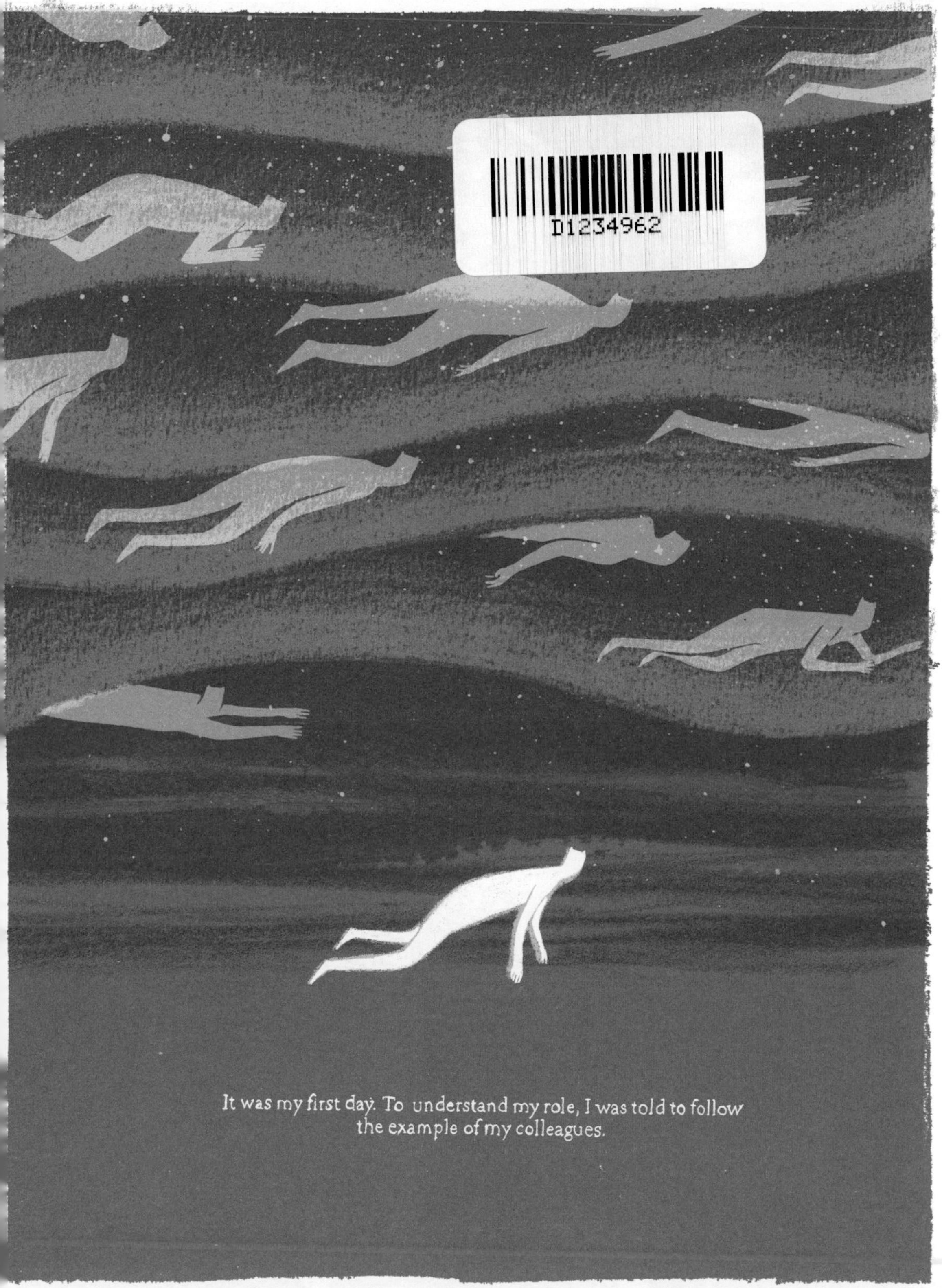
It was my first day. To understand my role, I was told to follow the example of my colleagues.

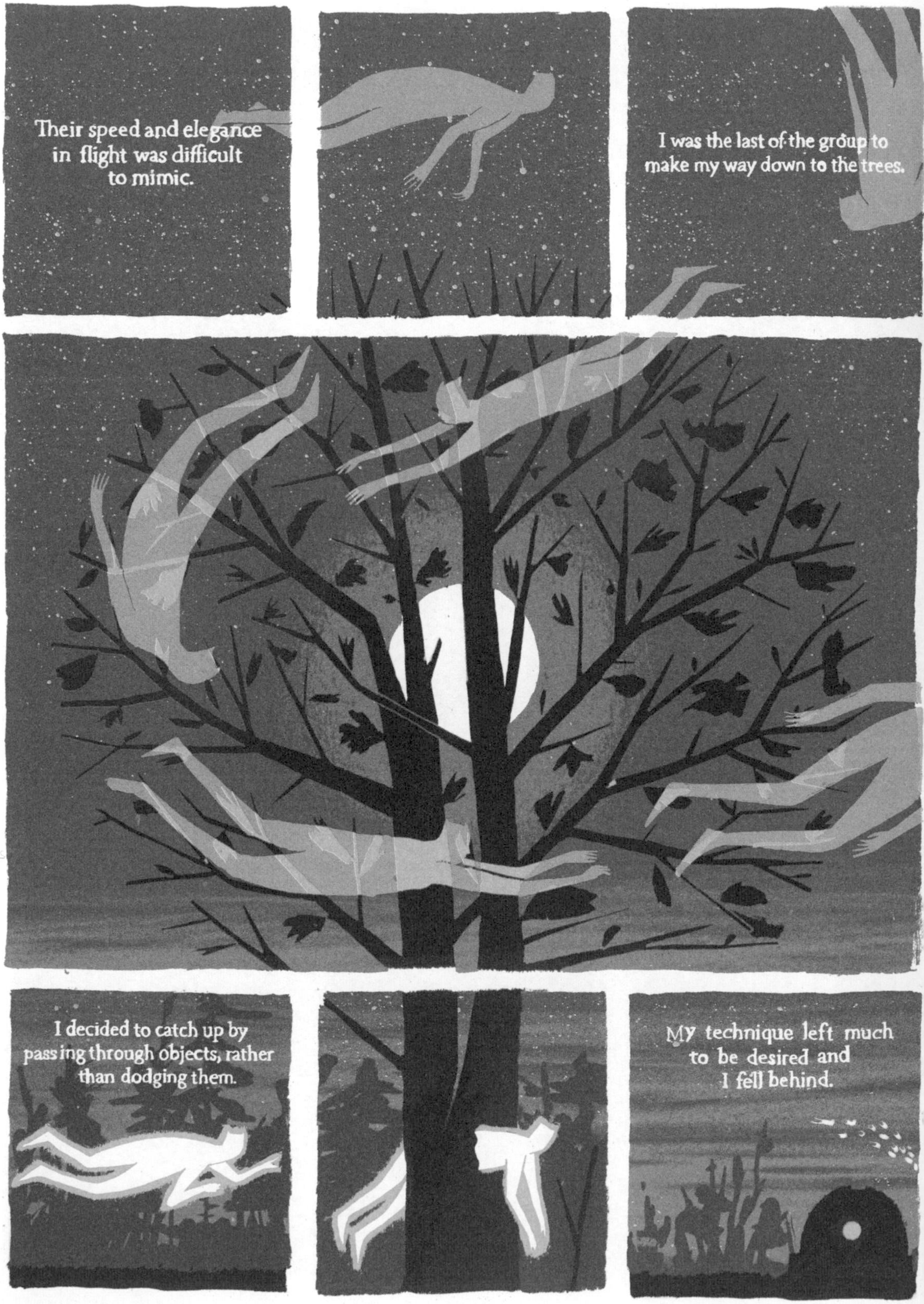
Their speed and elegance in flight was difficult to mimic.
I was the last of the group to make my way down to the trees.
I decided to catch up by passing through objects, rather than dodging them.
My technique left much to be desired and I fell behind.

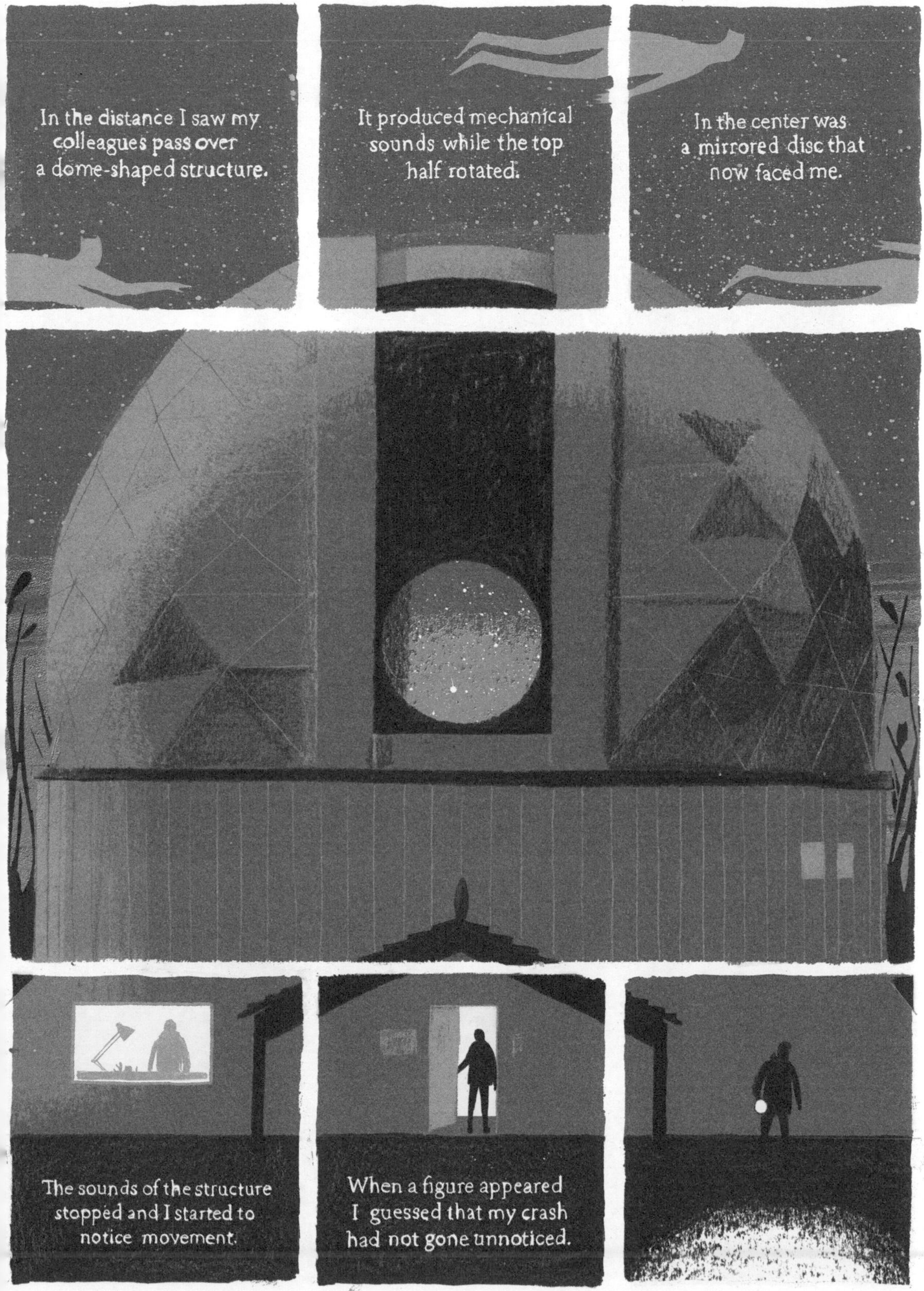
In the distance I saw my colleagues pass over a dome-shaped structure.
It produced mechanical sounds while the top half rotated.
In the center was a mirrored disc that now faced me.
The sounds of the structure stopped and I started to notice movement.
When a figure appeared I guessed that my crash had not gone unnoticed.

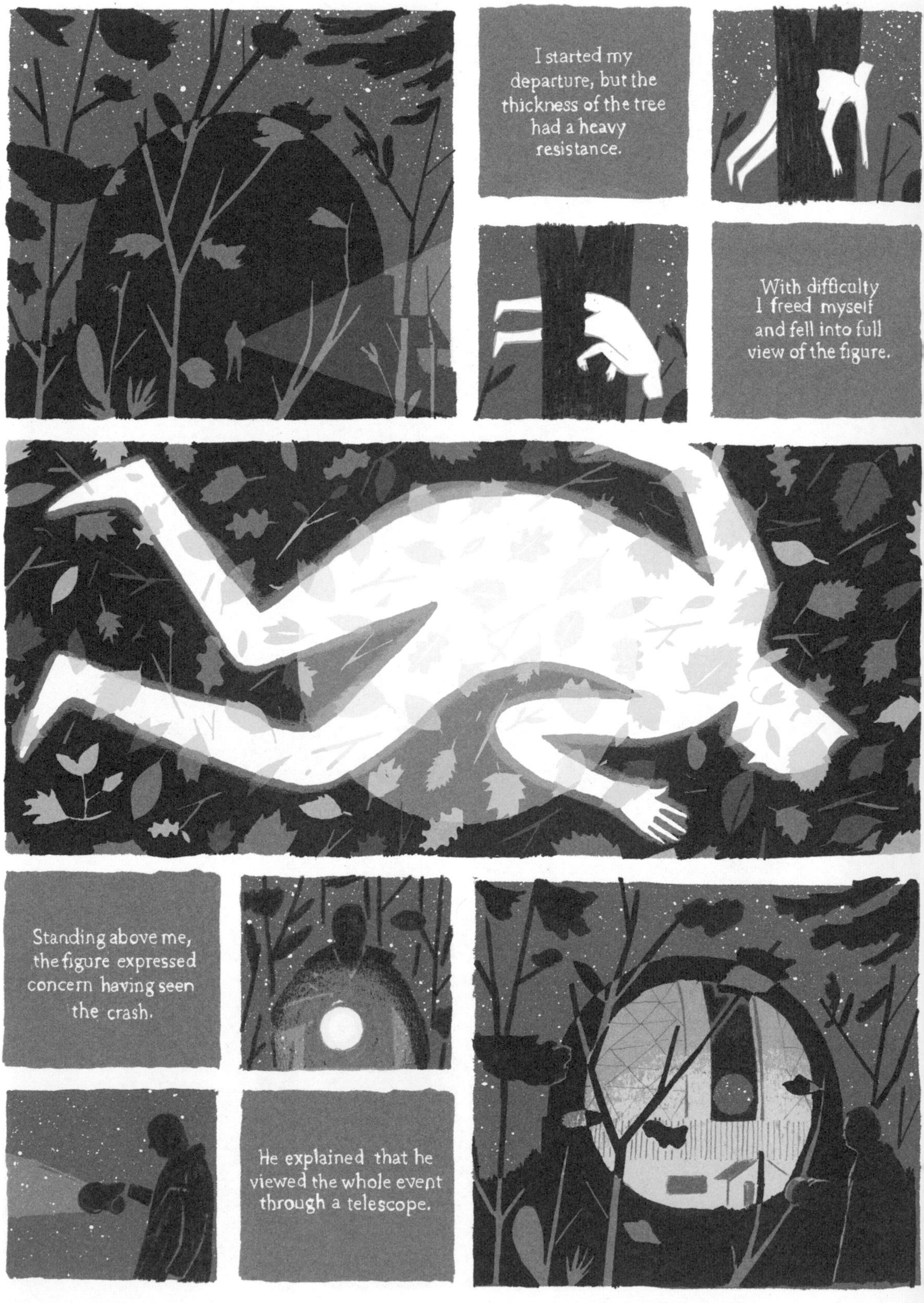
I started my departure, but the thickness of the tree had a heavy resistance.
With difficulty I freed myself and fell into full view of the figure.
Standing above me, the figure expressed concern having seen the crash.
He explained that he viewed the whole event through a telescope.

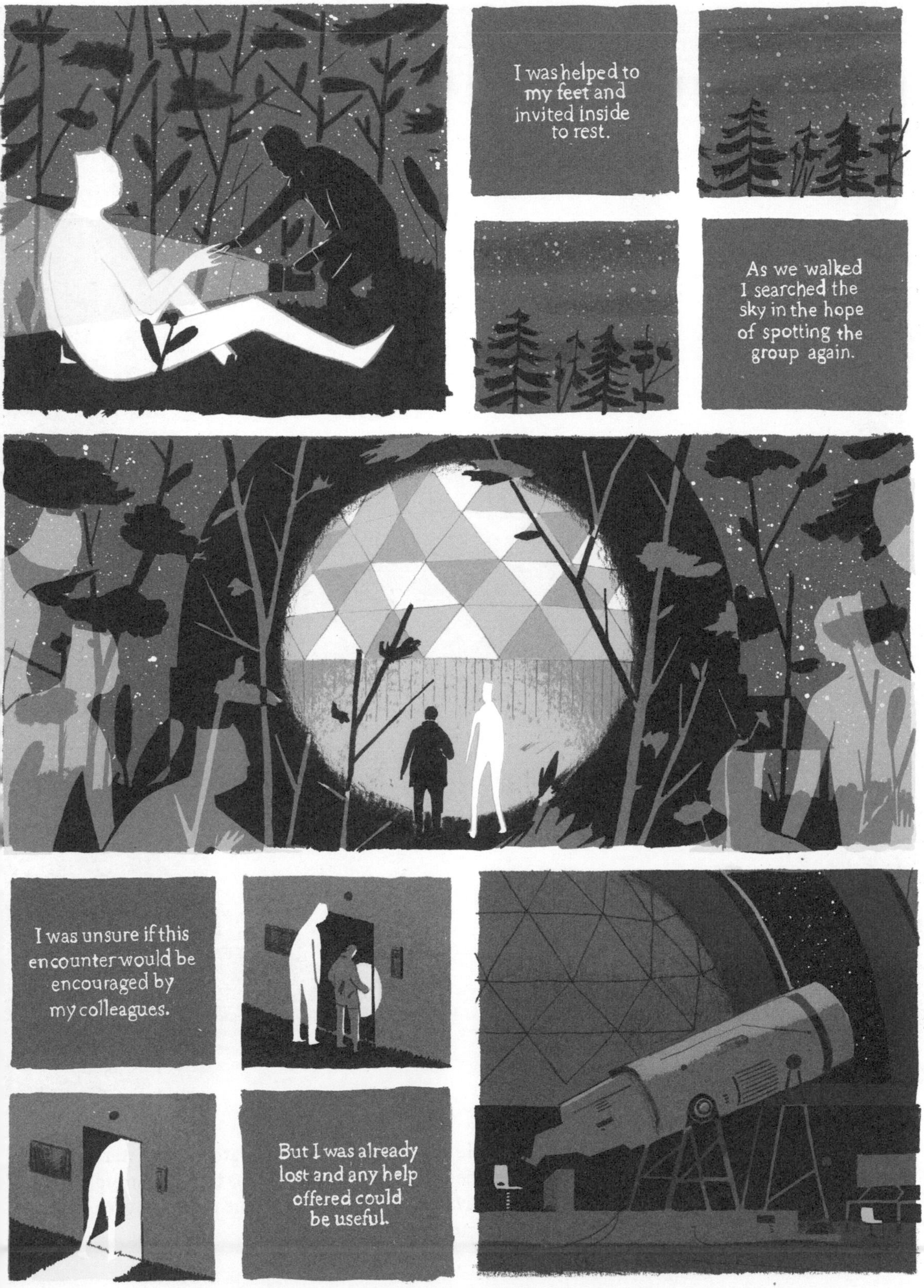
I was helped to my feet and invited inside to rest.
As we walked I searched the sky in the hope of spotting the group again.
I was unsure if this encounter would be encouraged by my colleagues.
But I was already lost and any help offered could be useful.

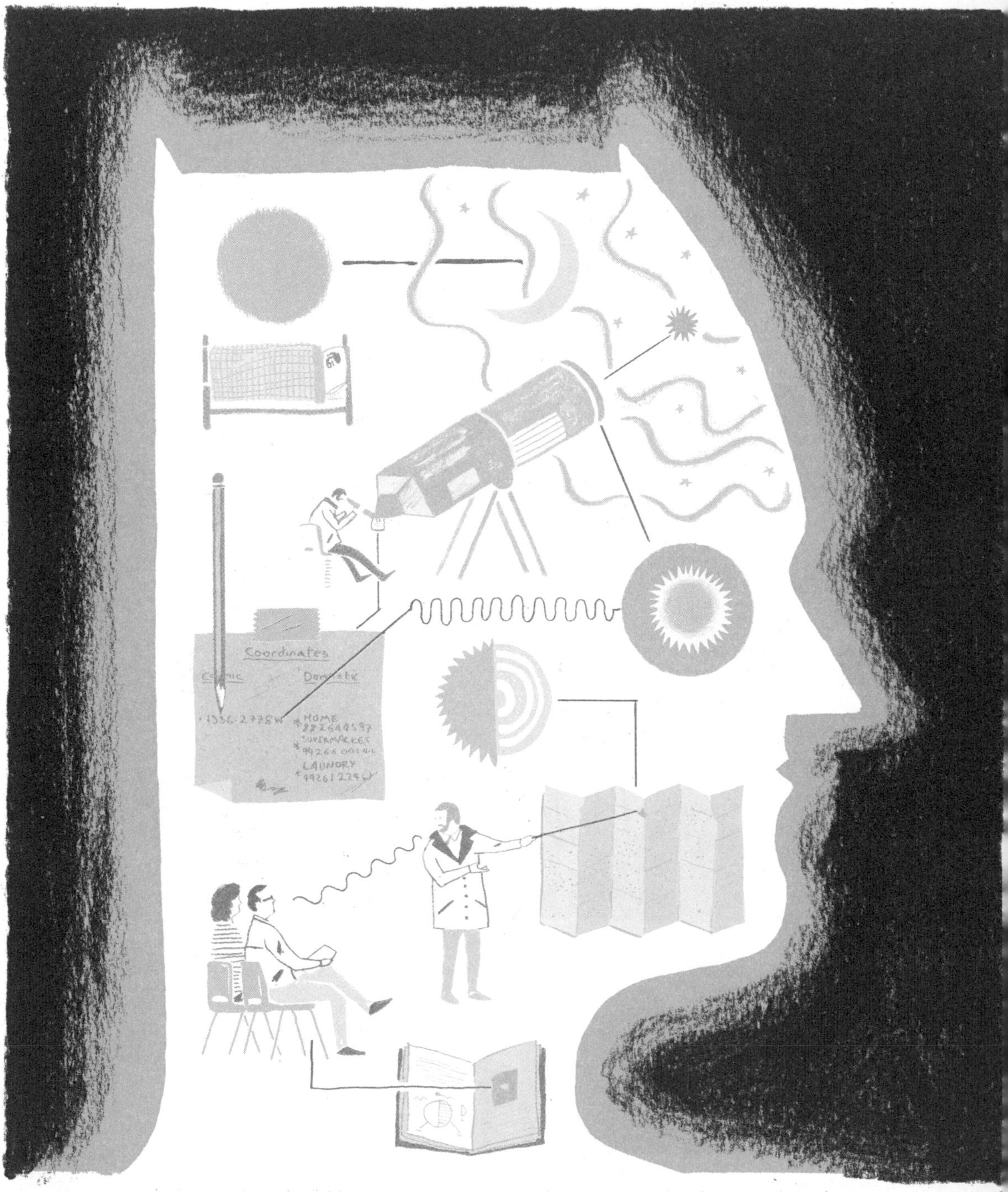
Coordinates
HOME
SUPERMARKET
LAUNDRY

Once inside, I could see that the figure was a man. He explained that he was watching the stars through the telescope when my group and I flew past. I learned that the man's work was to look through the telescope and study the stars all night, leaving his days to rest. He hoped to one day discover a new star, learn how it was born and have the work presented and published.

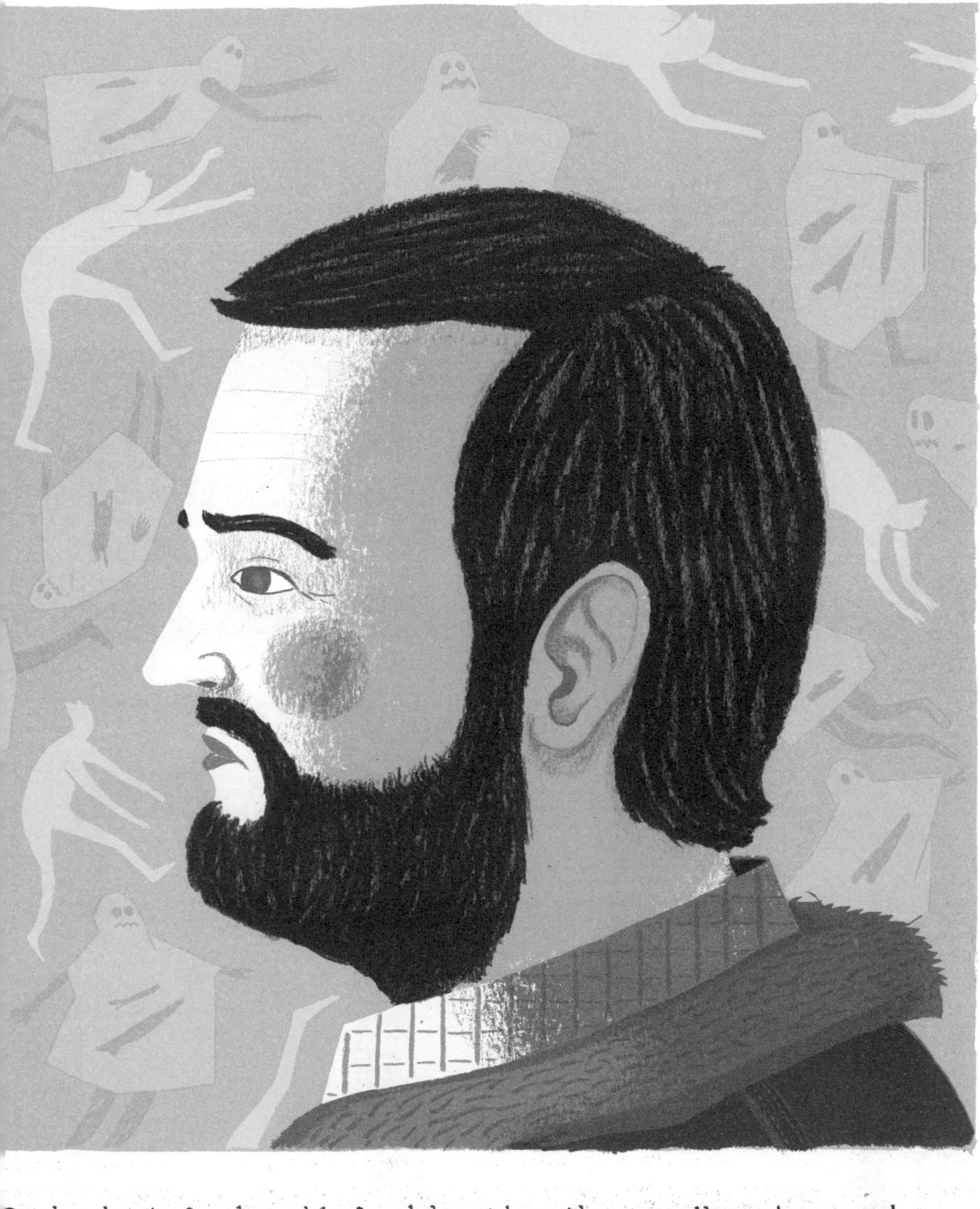

I made it clear that I was lost and that I needed to catch up with my group. Unsure about my task, or the activities of my colleagues, I didn't have much direction. The man had a few vague suggestions about "haunting" but I was sure there was more to my work than that. The man kindly offered his help and equipment but insisted I wear a daytime disguise.

As the morning light set in, the man began collecting spare clothing and portable telescopes for the search.

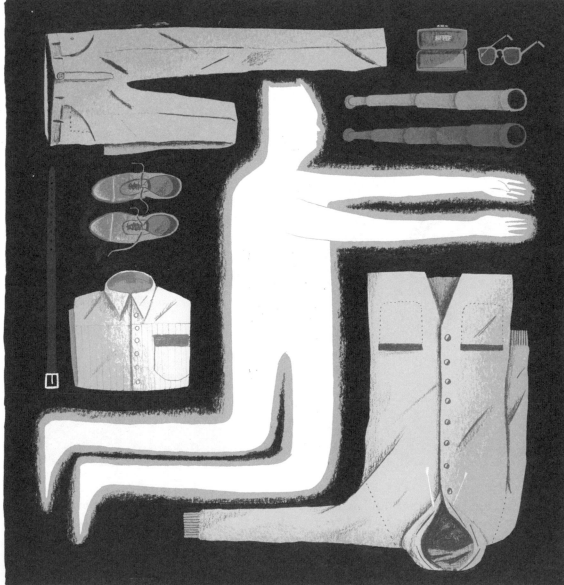

Deciding that the town would be a good place to start our search, we set off.

As we looked, the man pointed out areas of town he enjoyed most.

I started to doubt his concentration until he noticed a flying figure.

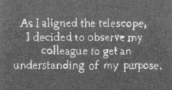

As I aligned the telescope, I decided to observe my colleague to get an understanding of my purpose.

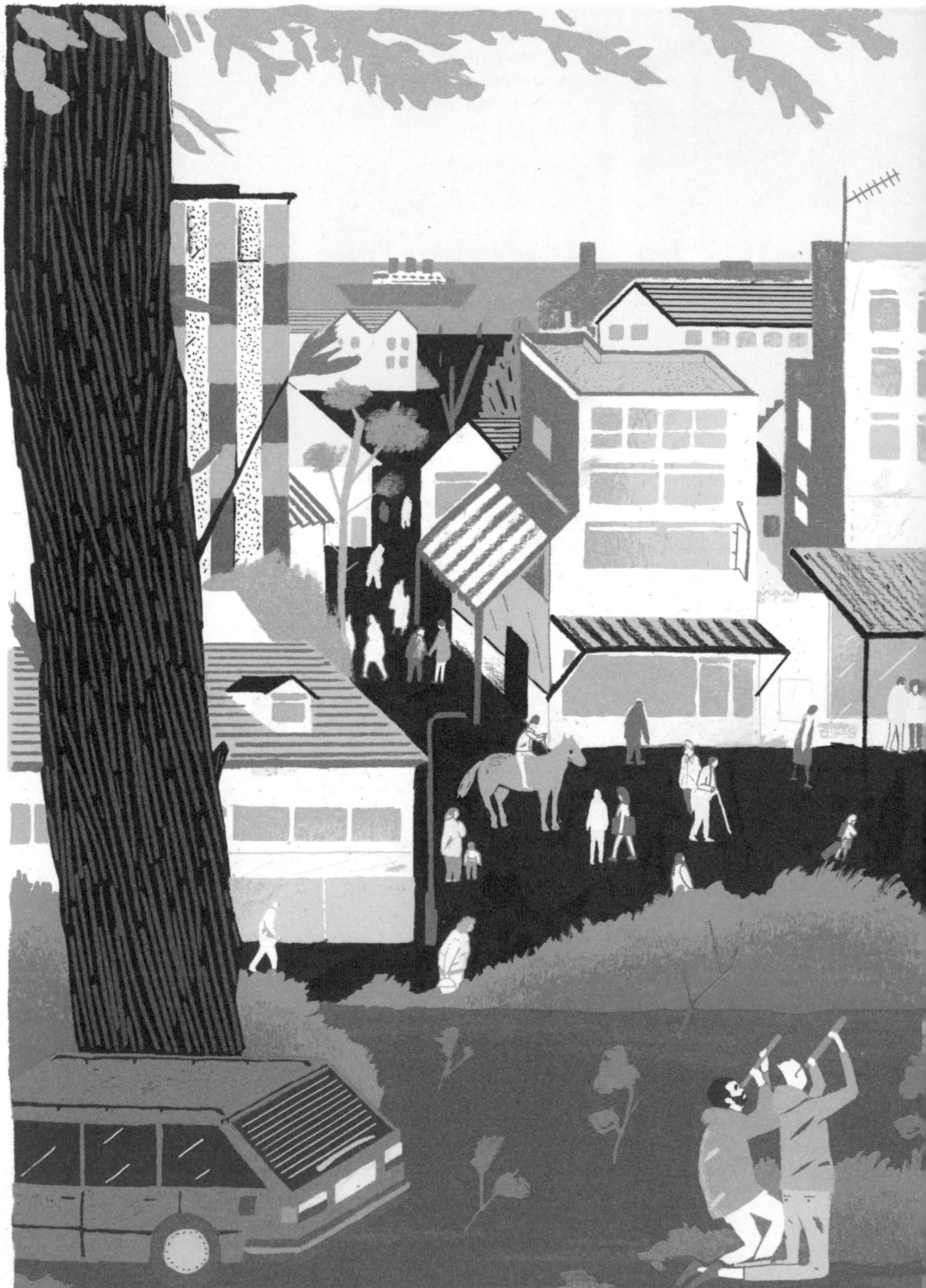

Over residential rooftops, the translucent figure dropped down.

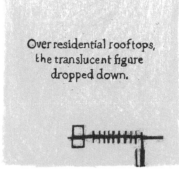

A subtle and precise entrance was made.

I could faintly hear music from the open window.

The sound seemed to attract my colleague closer

to a woman who was creating it.

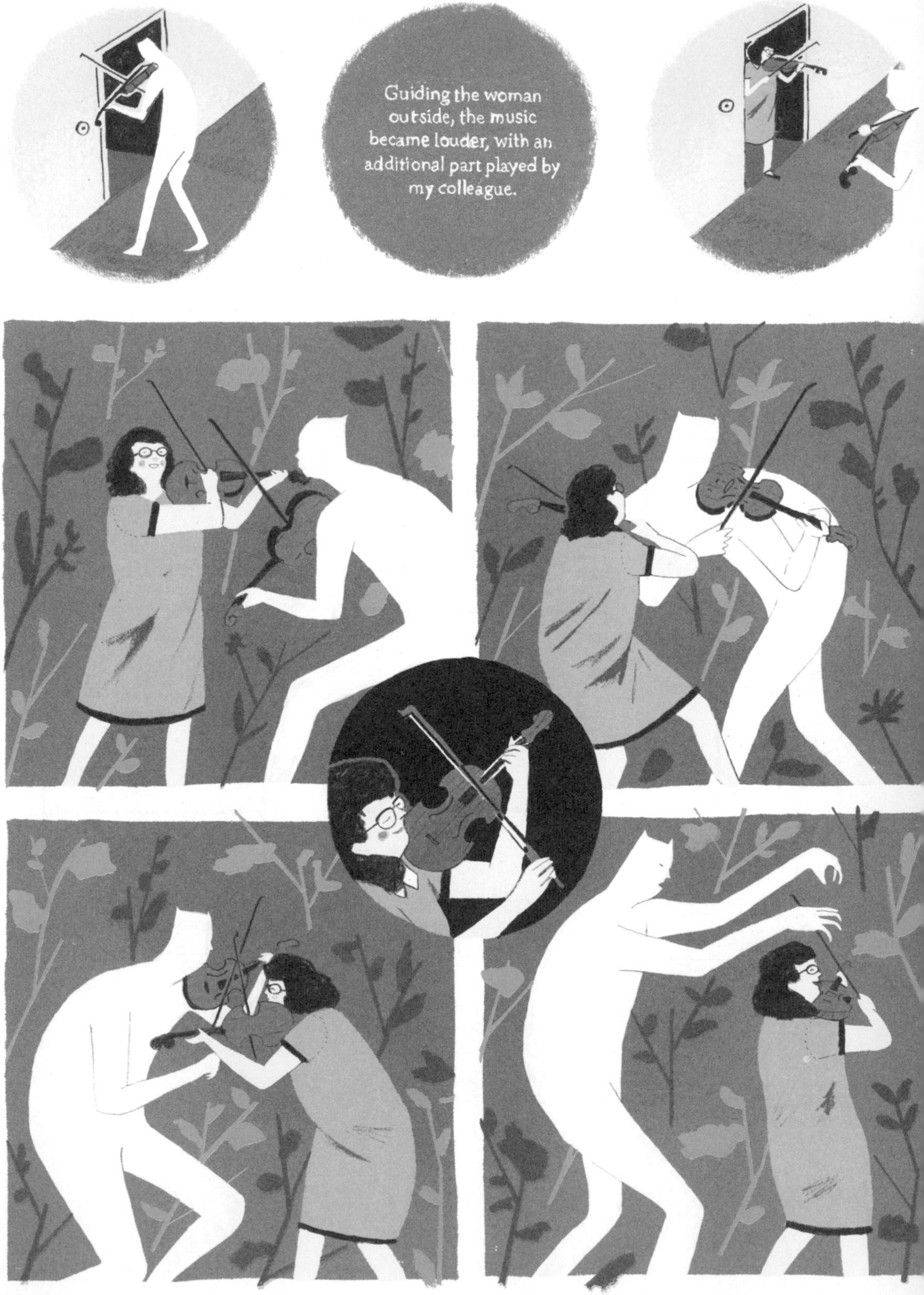
Guiding the woman outside, the music became louder, with an additional part played by my colleague.

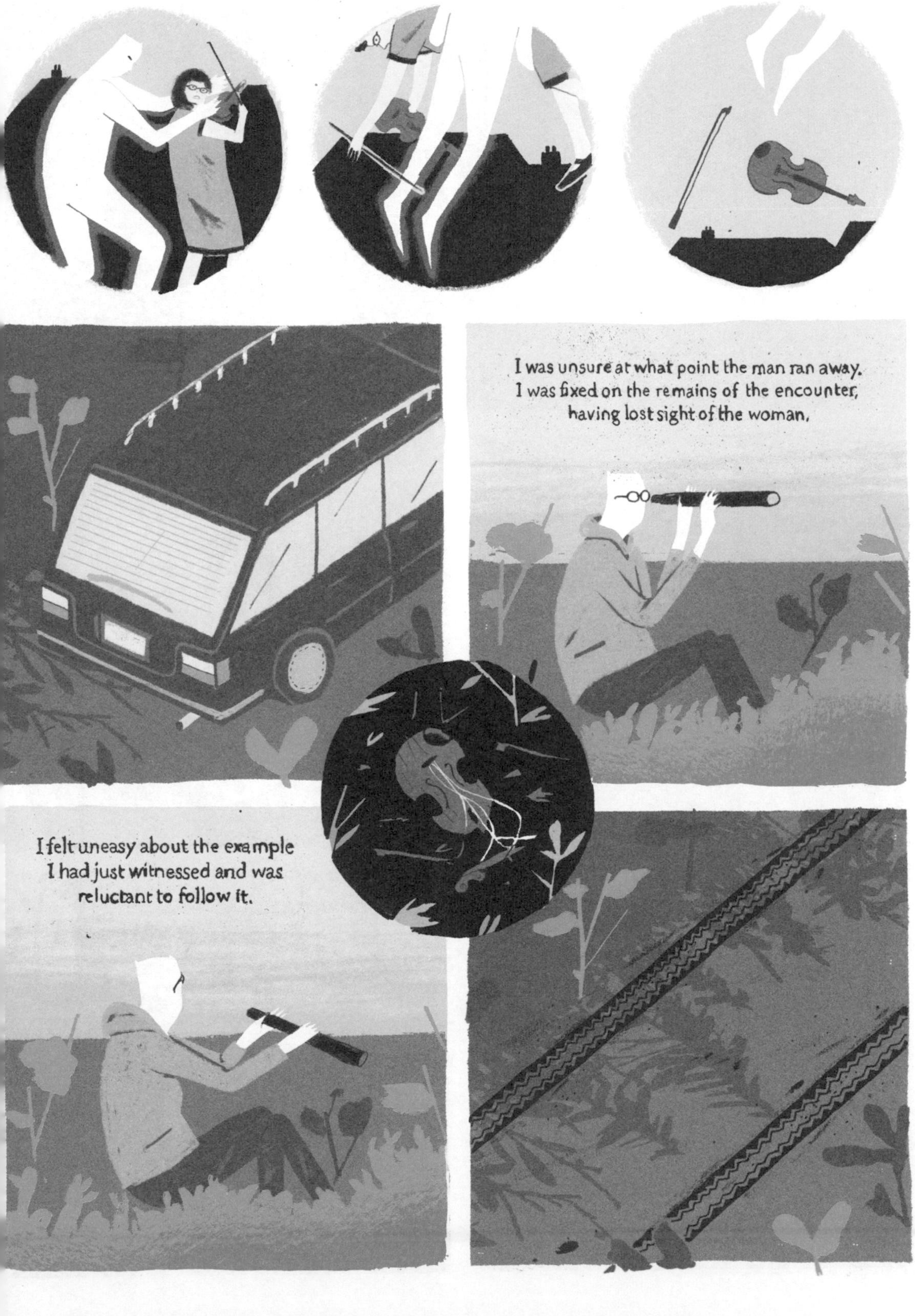
I was unsure at what point the man ran away.
I was fixed on the remains of the encounter,
having lost sight of the woman.
I felt uneasy about the example
I had just witnessed and was
reluctant to follow it.

I followed the tracks.
I wanted to find the man
and speak to him.

Explain that I was no danger
to him.

Losing the trail, I noticed
a familiar structure
through the trees.

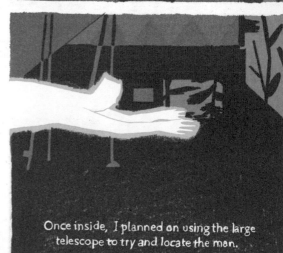

With no sight of the man or his vehicle I slowly
entered the building.

Once inside, I planned on using the large
telescope to try and locate the man.

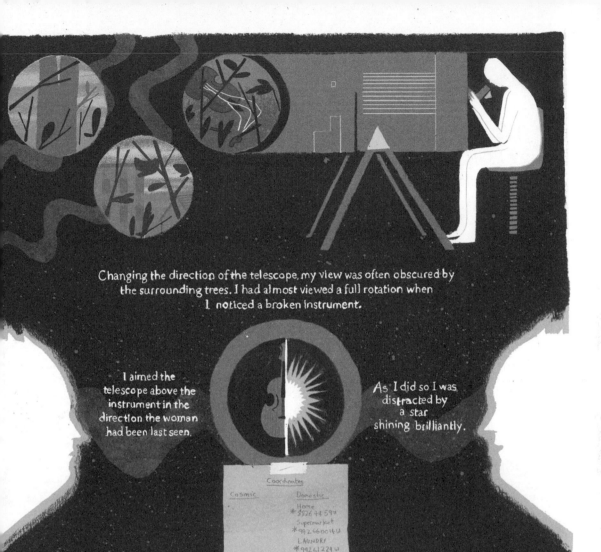

Changing the direction of the telescope, my view was often obscured by the surrounding trees. I had almost viewed a full rotation when I noticed a broken instrument.

I aimed the telescope above the instrument in the direction the woman had been last seen.

As I did so I was distracted by a star shining brilliantly.

Coordinates

Cosmic   Domestic
                Home
                *982641597
                Supermarket
                *992660014u
                LAUNDRY
                *992612294u

I greatly admired the man's work and thought it was a much more appealing job. Attached to the viewfinder was a handwritten list of co-ordinates. One set was labelled "home," so I adjusted the dials.

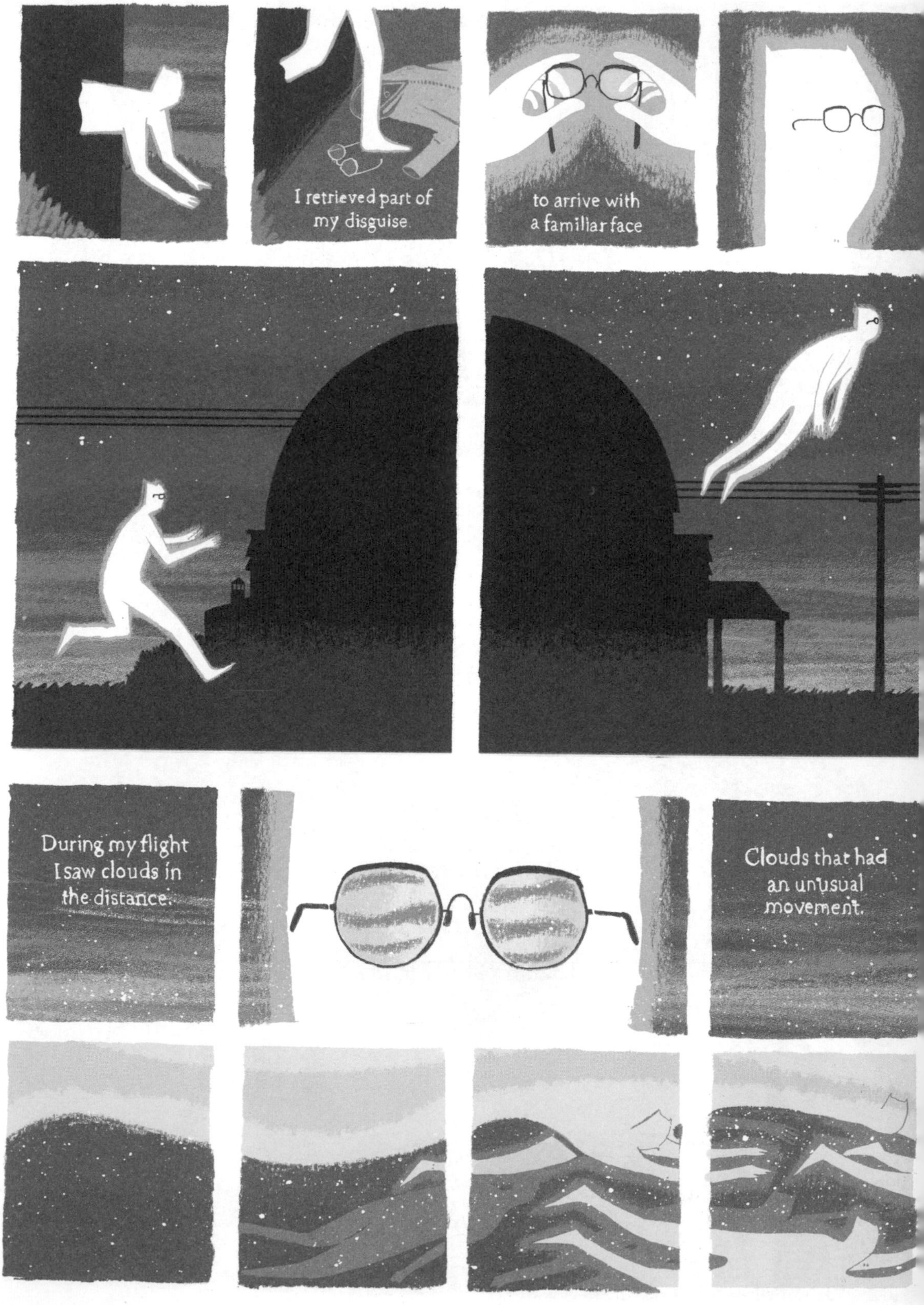
I retrieved part of my disguise
to arrive with a familiar face
During my flight I saw clouds in the distance.
Clouds that had an unusual movement.

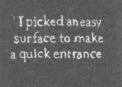

I picked an easy
surface to make
a quick entrance

and found the
man asleep at
his desk.

As soon as the man awoke, I started apologising before he had time to react.

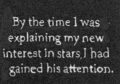

By the time I was explaining my new interest in stars, I had gained his attention.

My carelessness with the man's possession had allowed me to be tracked.

I apologised again for the threat I had now brought to his home.

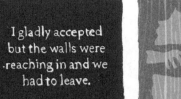
He invited me to work with him to help explore the birth of stars.

I gladly accepted but the walls were reaching in and we had to leave.

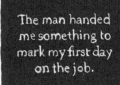

The man handed me something to mark my first day on the job.

A gift of a new set for the beginning of a new profession.

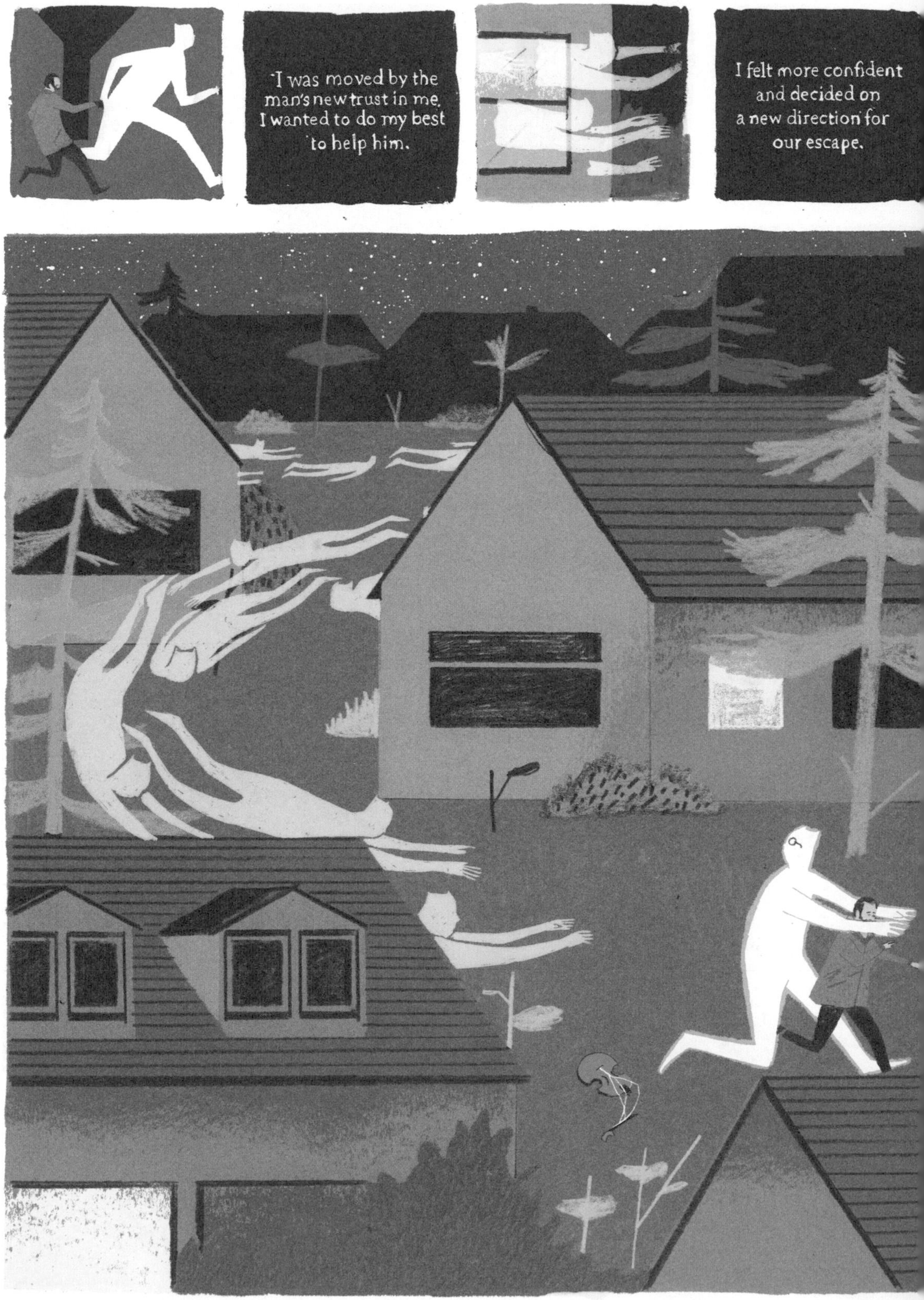
I was moved by the man's new trust in me. I wanted to do my best to help him.
I felt more confident and decided on a new direction for our escape.

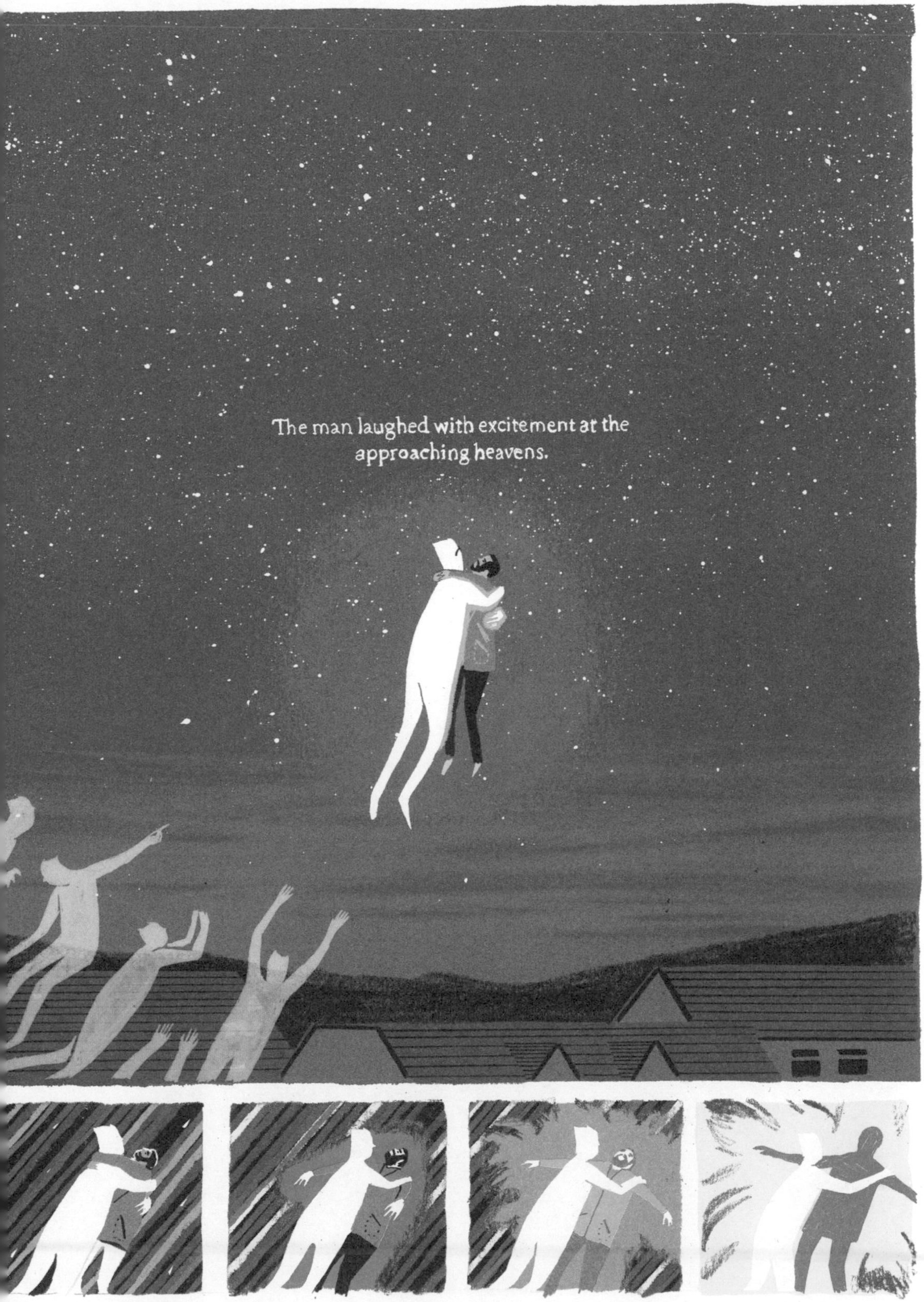
The man laughed with excitement at the approaching heavens.

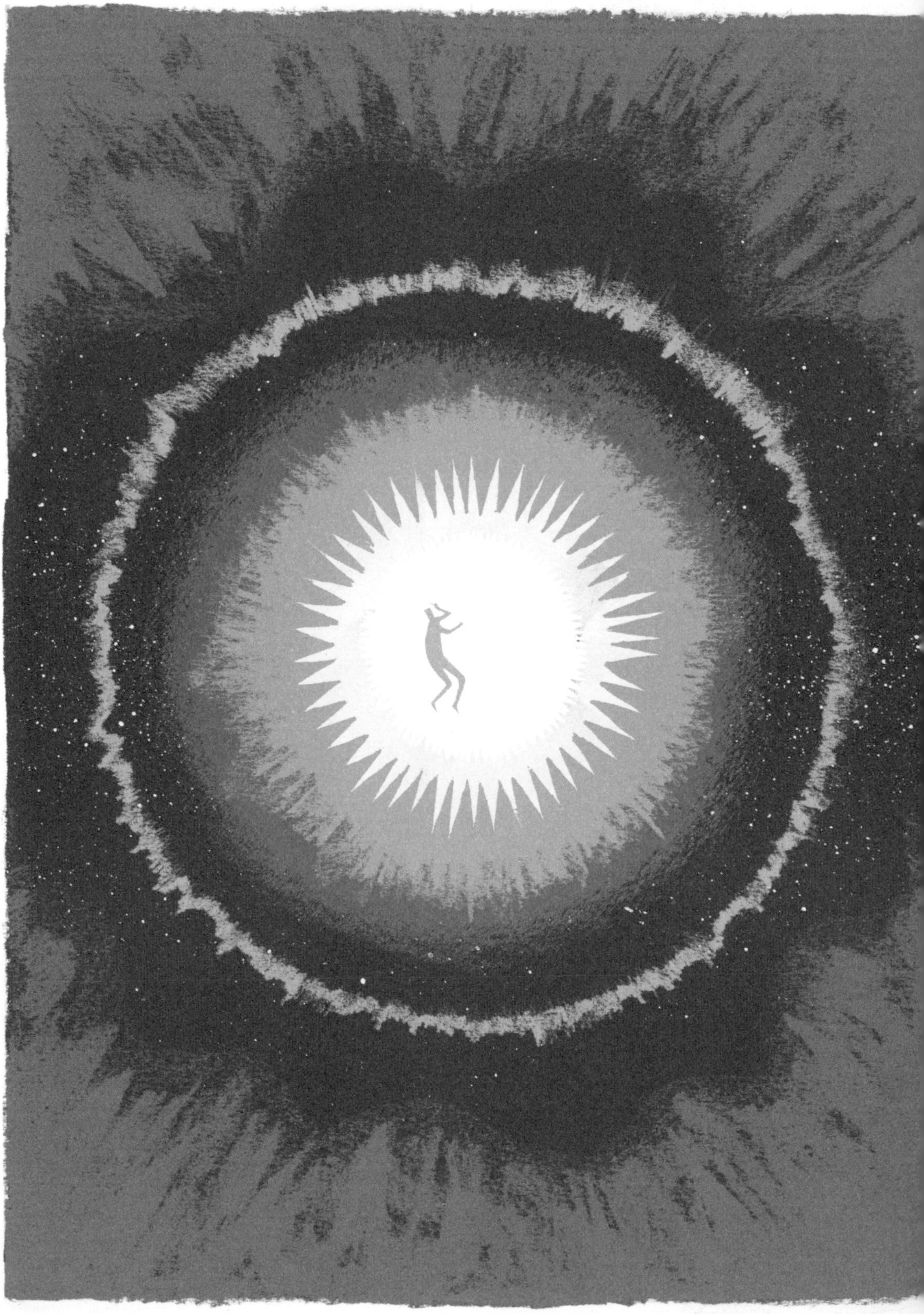

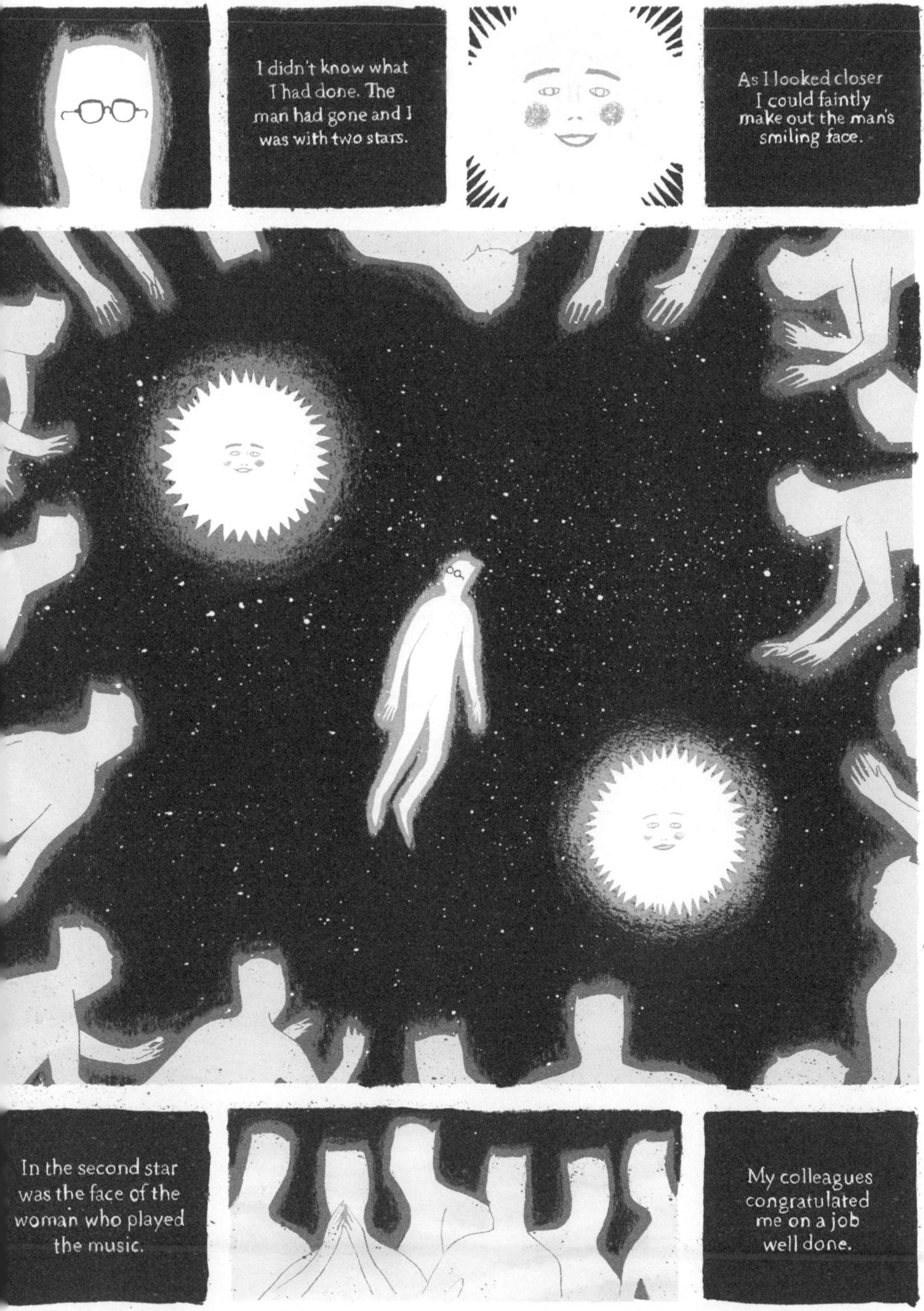
I didn't know what I had done. The man had gone and I was with two stars.
As I looked closer I could faintly make out the man's smiling face.
In the second star was the face of the woman who played the music.
My colleagues congratulated me on a job well done.

until then they would have to wait and see.

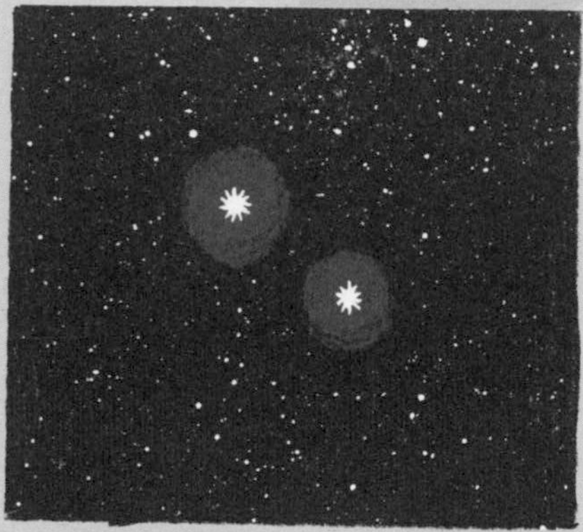

New Stars Thom and Nellie

Last night a town local discovered two new stars. The stars have been named Thom and Nellie and are set to be registered and published in the next editions of astronomical catalogues.